Pebble®
Plus

(EXPLORE
LIFE CYCLES)

An Apple Tree's
Life Cycle

by Mary R. Dunn

CAPSTONE PRESS
a capstone imprint

Pebble Plus is published by Capstone Press,
1710 Roe Crest Drive, North Mankato, Minnesota 56003
www.mycapstone.com

Library of Congress Cataloging-in-Publication Data
Library of Congress Cataloging-in-Publication data is available on the Library of Congress
website.
ISBN 978-1-5157-7055-8 (library binding)
ISBN 978-1-5157-7061-9 (paperback)
ISBN 978-1-5157-7067-1 (eBook PDF)

Editorial Credits
Anna Butzer, editor; Kyle Grenz, designer
Wanda Winch, media researcher; Kathy McColley, production specialist

Photo Credits
Dreamstime: Deepspacedave, 7; Shutterstock: Adriana Nikolova, 21, branislavpudar, 19,
gorillaimages, 13, Helga42, 15, images72, back cover, 5, Michaela Steininger, cover, Nikohm
Kedban, 3, 6, 8, 12, 24, Nosyrevy, 10, 14, November Oscar Kilo, 17, Robert Schneider, 11, Zoom
Team, 1; Thinkstock: iStockphoto/Forester_, 9

Note to Parents and Teachers

The Explore Life Cycles set supports national science standards related to life science. This
book describes and illustrates the life cycle of apple trees. The images support early readers in
understanding the text. The repetition of words and phrases helps early readers learn new words.
This book also introduces early readers to subject-specific vocabulary words, which are defined in
the Glossary section. Early readers may need assistance to read some words and to use the Table of
Contents, Glossary, Read More, Internet Sites, Critical Thinking Questions, and Index sections
of the book.

Printed and bound in the USA.
060619 002230

Table of Contents

Planting Seeds in Spring

Apples are a delicious, juicy fruit.

Yum! They grow on trees.

There are about 7,500 kinds

of apple trees.

Many apple trees start as tiny seeds.
After the seed is planted,
roots grow. Next, a shoot
pushes up out of the ground.

Leaves begin to grow.

The shoot becomes a seedling.

In two years, the plant is a sapling.

It is stronger and its trunk is getting thick.

A Red Delicious apple tree is full grown in 6 to 10 years. An adult tree can grow to be 25 feet (7.6 meters) tall. Each spring, bright blossoms grow with the leaves.

Blossoms have stamens full of pollen. Blossoms also have nectar, a sweet juice bees like. Bees fly from blossom to blossom to drink the nectar.

Pollen dust sticks on bees'
hairy legs. They carry it
from one blossom to another.
Pollen helps to make new
apple seeds.

Growing Fruit in Summer

Small apples grow where the blossoms used to be. The apples get bigger and tastier. Two hundred apples may grow on one tree.

Picking Fruit in Fall

In fall, ripe apples are picked for selling.

Apple trees' leaves turn red and yellow

and fall to the ground.

The trees are bare. But branches

are covered with tight buds.

Apple Trees in Winter

Trees rest during cold months.
In spring, the buds open and
the life cycle begins again.

GLOSSARY

blossom—a flower on a fruit tree or other plant

bud—a small shoot on a plant that grows into a leaf or a flower

nectar—a sweet liquid found in many flowers

pollen—a powder made by flowers to help them create new seeds

ripe—ready to pick and eat

root—the part of the plant that is underground

shoot—the white stem growing out of a seed that becomes a plant

stamen—the male part of the flower that makes pollen

READ MORE

Bulla, Clyde Robert. *A Tree Is a Plant.* Let's Read and Find Out Science. New York: Harper Collins, 2016.

George, Gale. *The Life Cycle of a Maple Tree.* Watch Them Grow! New York: PowerKids Press, 2015.

Rockwell, Anne. *Apples and Pumpkins.* New York: Aladdin, 2012.

INTERNET SITES

FactHound offers a safe, fun way to find Internet sites related to this book. All of the sites on FactHound have been researched by our staff.

Here's all you do:

Visit *www.facthound.com*

Type in this code: 9781515770558

 Check out projects, games and lots more at **www.capstonekids.com**

CRITICAL THINKING QUESTIONS

1. Why do bees fly from apple tree to apple tree?

2. We can see most parts of an apple tree.
   What part of an apple tree is below the ground?

INDEX